# It's all about…
# REMARKABLE
# ROMANS

KINGFISHER

D0626487

**KINGFISHER**

First published 2017 by Kingfisher
An imprint of Macmillan Children's Books
20 New Wharf Road, London N1 9RR
Associated companies throughout the world
www.panmacmillan.com

Series editor: Sarah Snashall
Series design: Anthony Hannant (LittleRedAnt)
Adapted from an original text by Philip Steele

ISBN 978-0-7534-3935-7

Printed in China

9 8 7 6 5 4 3 2 1

1TR/0716/WKT/UG/128MA

A CIP catalogue record for this book is available from the British Library.

Picture credits
The Publisher would like to thank the following for permission to reproduce their material.
Top = t; Bottom = b; Centre = c; Left = l; Right = r
Cover Alamy/David Cole; back cover iStock/claudiodivizia; pages 1 Alamy/David Cole;
2–3 Shutterstock/Mapics; 4 Shutterstock/Bertl123; 5 Shutterstock/oksmit; 5c Musée de Laon/
Vassil; 6 iStock/Duncan Walker; 6b Shutterstock/saiko3p; 7 Shutterstock/Brian Maudsley;
7t iStock/Cristofolux; 8 iStock/JSSIII; 8c iStock/David Ward; 9b, 10, 12 Kingfisher Artbank;
11 iStock/AndreaAstes; 11t iStock/Hedda Gjerpen; 12b Getty/DEA/M Carrieri; 13 Shutterstock/
Luciano Mortula; 13c Shutterstock/Mapics; 14–15 Shutterstock/Leonid Andronov;
16–17 Kingfisher Artbank; 17t Crodrin.B; 18l Alamy/Lanmas; 18r Joanbanjo; 19l Walters Art
Museum; 19r Kingfisher Artbank; 20 iStock/Sami Suni; 21t Shutterstock/muratart;
21b Shutterstock/meunierd; 22 iStock/BrettCharlton; 23 iStock; 23t Walters Art Museum;
24 Alamy/Mr Steve Vidler; 25 Jastrow; 25b Alamy/Art Archive; 26–27 iStock/roc8jas; 26b Greg
Willis; 27 Shutterstock/S-F; 28–29 Alamy/APS(UK); 29 Kingfisher Artbank; 30–31 Shutterstock/
Mapics; 32 iStock/ArevHamb.
Cards: Front tl iStock/Gabriele Maltini; tr Shutterstock/Luciano Mortula; bl Shutterstock/Honzr
Hruby; br Shutterstock/WitR; Back tl iStock/allou; tr Shutterstock/Benedictus; bl iStock;
br Shutterstock/Reinhold Leitner.

You will find c. before some dates. This stands for *circa*, which means 'about'.

Front cover: The head of the goddess Sulis Minerva from the Temple Courtyard of
the Roman baths in Bath, UK.

# CONTENTS

# Who were the Romans?

The Romans were the people who ruled a huge empire almost 2000 years ago. With the help of their armies they spread their culture, language (Latin), building style and systems of organization.

## SPOTLIGHT: Roman Empire

| | |
|---|---|
| **Founded:** | 753BCE |
| **Ended:** | 476CE |
| **Language:** | Latin |
| **Location:** | centred on modern-day Italy |

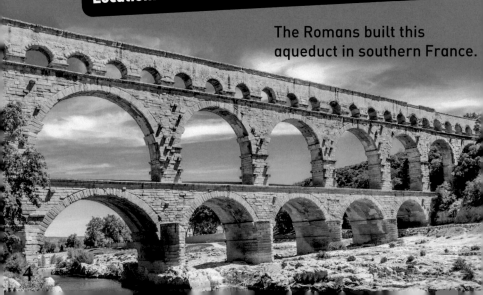

The Romans built this aqueduct in southern France.

4

Today we can still find the remains of Roman walls and buildings – even public baths. We sometimes dig up old coins, pottery jars or rings and brooches. These objects help us to understand how the Romans lived.

Elaborate jewellery, such as this pair of earrings, has been found at Roman sites.

Roman ruins near the town of Cordoba, in Spain.

# Rome and its empire

More than 2700 years ago Rome was just a few villages. By 1CE, Rome was the biggest city in the world. By 117CE, Rome ruled an empire that covered Spain, France, Britain, parts of Germany, Romania, Greece, western Asia and North Africa.

The Basilica Cistern in Constantinople (modern Istanbul) was built by the Roman Emperor Justinian.

Augustus changed the way Rome was ruled and became the first Roman emperor.

**SPOTLIGHT:** *Emperor Augustus*

**Born:** 63BCE (as Gaius Octavius)
**Died:** 14CE
**Ruled:** 27BCE – 14CE
**Famous for:** first emperor of Rome

The Romans built straight roads across their empire.

# FACT...

Legend says that Rome was founded by Romulus who, with his twin brother Remus, had been brought up by a wolf.

# Buying and selling

Every Roman city had a central place called the Forum. People met here to do business and to visit the market and shops.

Romans used coins made of gold, silver, bronze and copper.

The remains of the Forum in Rome.

The Romans were great traders. At Roman ports, ships were loaded with pottery and cloth. Traders bought and sold sacks of grain, jars of wine, olive oil and even people. These people were slaves who had no freedom and had to work hard for no money.

## FACT...

In 68BCE pirates attacked the Roman port of Ostia. The Romans built 500 ships to fight them.

# A mighty army

The Roman army was divided into groups called legions. Most soldiers fought on foot, but some fought on horseback. Roman soldiers wore tunics, sandals or boots, helmets and body armour. Their weapons were short swords, daggers and spears.

**Soldiers in the Roman army fought battles in strict and highly organized formations.**

a Roman general's helmet

One of the greatest Roman soldiers was the politician and general Julius Caesar. He became dictator of Rome before his enemies murdered him.

Julius Caesar marched into Rome and took over the government.

11

# Gods and temples

The Romans believed in many different gods including Jupiter (god of the sky), Juno (goddess of marriage), Diana (goddess of hunting) and Mars (god of war).

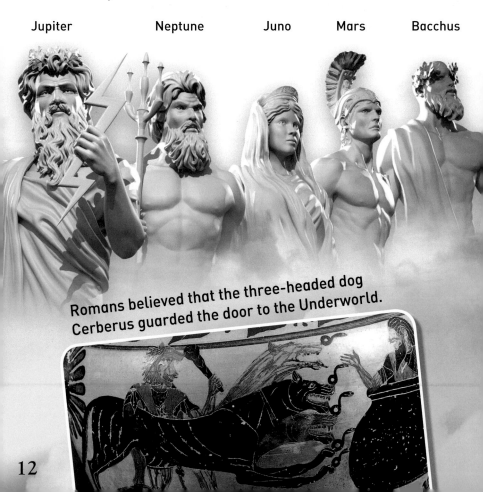

Jupiter          Neptune          Juno          Mars          Bacchus

Romans believed that the three-headed dog Cerberus guarded the door to the Underworld.

The Romans built temples and held festivals to honour their gods, and told myths about them. These stories also told of heroes and monsters.

SPOTLIGHT: Pantheon

**Built for:** dedicated to all the gods
**When:** 118 – 125CE
**Built by:** Emperor Hadrian
**Famous for:** having a huge concrete dome

The Pantheon Temple, Rome. Its domed ceiling (below) is nearly 2000 years old.

M·AGRIPPA·L·F·COS·TERTIVM

# At home

The Romans built different kinds of houses. In the biggest cities, such as Rome or Ostia, people lived in blocks of flats. Many towns had family houses with a tiled roof, open courtyard and pools of water. The small windows had shutters.

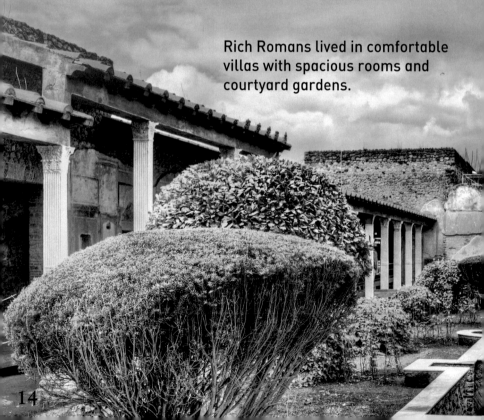

Rich Romans lived in comfortable villas with spacious rooms and courtyard gardens.

In the country, rich people owned big houses called villas. Some had fine wall paintings, called frescoes, or floors decorated with mosaics.

## FACT...

Romans believed that gods and spirits protected their homes. People made offerings to these gods every day.

# Food and feasts

In the kitchens of the rich, slaves carried water and firewood. Pots and pans boiled on the brick stove. Cooks used olive oil, herbs and spices. A main dish might be pork, fish or chicken. Roman people ate onions, peas and cabbages, as well as figs and grapes. They sweetened their food and drinks with honey.

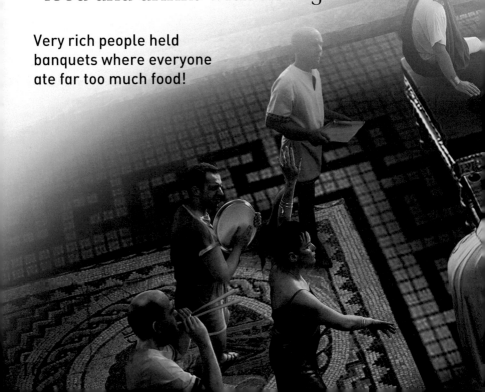

Very rich people held banquets where everyone ate far too much food!

# FACT...

Guests at a Roman banquet might eat mice cooked in honey, snails in wine, dumplings made with brains or even boiled ostrich.

Wealthy Romans used silver tableware, while others used utensils made from bone or wood.

# Getting dressed

A rich Roman woman would wear a long tunic with a woollen dress called a stola on top. She would use perfume and jars of make-up, and curl her hair and pile it up in the latest hairstyle. She would check her appearance in a mirror made of polished metal.

Rich women would have bronze mirrors and wooden combs.

Important men wore a heavy woollen robe called a toga. They wrapped it around themselves and then over one shoulder. Children, slaves and working people all wore short tunics.

# FACT...

Wealthy Roman women covered their face with poisonous white lead to make themselves look pale.

Jewellery, such as this snake bracelet, was made from gold, pearls and precious stones.

# Thrills and spills

The Romans loved to watch violent and dangerous sports. At the Circus Maximus stadium in Rome they could watch exciting chariot racing. At the Colosseum slaves and gladiators battled each other to the death. There were also wild animal fights and mock sea battles.

**SPOTLIGHT:** Colosseum, Rome

| | |
|---|---|
| **Built:** | 72–80CE |
| **Height:** | 50 m |
| **Capacity:** | 50,000 people |
| **Famous for:** | the arena had 36 trap doors |

Romans who wanted less bloodthirsty entertainment could enjoy funny plays (comedies) or sad ones (tragedies) at the theatre.

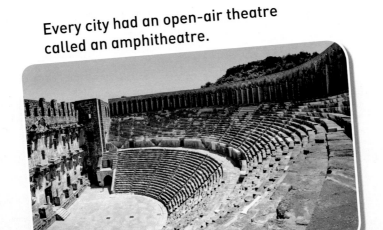

Every city had an open-air theatre called an amphitheatre.

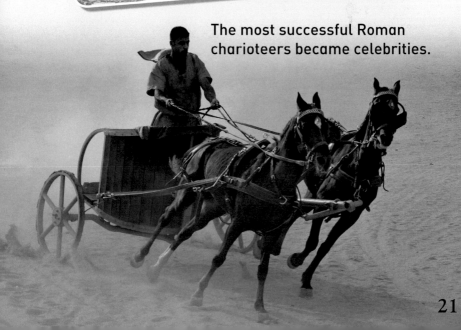

The most successful Roman charioteers became celebrities.

# Going to the baths

Every Roman town had public baths for men and women. Romans went there every day to meet their friends and relax. They often started with some exercises or games. Then they would visit the pools, the hot tubs, the cold tubs and steam rooms. Afterwards, they might have a massage.

The remains of Roman underfloor heating at Housesteads Roman fort, Northumberland.

# FACT...

At the baths, the Romans rubbed their body with oil and then scraped it clean with a tool called a strigil (right).

The Roman baths in Bath were built over a natural hot spring.

# Girls, boys and toys

Roman babies played with clay rattles in the shape of animals. Toddlers played with marbles and dolls. At about seven years old, some boys and girls learned reading, writing and arithmetic. They used a sharp point to scrape the letters on boards covered in wax. If they made a mistake, they smoothed over the wax and started again.

**Romans played different games with counters on a square board.**

Some boys from rich families learned about history, poetry and making speeches. Some girls learned how to run a home, how to sew and how to play a musical instrument.

a toy buffalo from Ancient Rome

# FACT...

At birth, Roman children were given a charm called a bulla. They wore it until they were 16 years old (boys) or married (girls).

# Pompeii

In 79CE, a volcano called Mount Vesuvius erupted with huge force. A cloud of super-heated ash and rock poured from the volcano and buried the nearby town of Pompeii.

## FACT...

The entrance of one house in Pompeii had a picture of a fierce dog with a notice saying 'Beware of the dog'.

## SPOTLIGHT: Pompeii

| | |
|---|---|
| **Buried:** | 79CE |
| **Rediscovered:** | 1748 by Spaniard, Alcubierre |
| **Population at time:** | 11,000 people |
| **Importance:** | preserved Roman town |

Hundreds of years later, the rock was cleared away and workers found the buried Roman streets, houses, shops, markets and theatres. They even found left-over food in pots and pans.

Many villas in Pompeii had colourful paintings on their walls.

# What happened to Rome?

The Romans fought their enemies for hundreds of years. The Roman Empire became huge, but it was difficult to rule. Warriors attacked the forts along its borders, and some even attacked the city of Rome. The city became less powerful and was finally taken over by armies from the north of Europe.

An aerial view of Housesteads Fort on Hadrian's Wall, the northernmost border of the Roman Empire.

# Important Dates in Ancient Rome

**753BCE**  Rome begins

**250BCE**  The Romans rule most of Italy

**58–50BCE** Julius Caesar conquers Gaul (including modern-day France)

**27BCE**  Augustus becomes first Roman Emperor

**43CE**  The Romans start to conquer Britain

**79CE**  The volcano Vesuvius erupts in Italy

**117CE**  The Roman Empire is at its largest

**330CE**  Constantinople becomes capital of the Roman Empire in the east

**410CE**  Goths attack and capture Rome

**476CE**  The Roman Empire in the west comes to an end

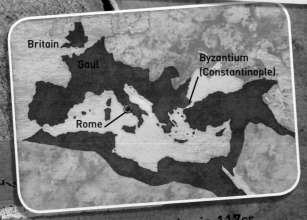

Britain

Gaul

Byzantium (Constantinople)

Rome

the Roman Empire in 117CE

# GLOSSARY

**aqueduct** A bridge that carries water.

BCE Short for 'Before the Common Era' (any date before 1CE). It is also sometimes known as BC (before Christ).

**chariot** A light, fast-moving carriage pulled by horses.

**conquer** To beat an enemy.

**culture** The ways of living of a particular group of people.

**empire** A group of countries ruled by one emperor.

**erupt** To explode violently.

**forum** The business centre and meeting place in an Ancient Roman town.

**legion** A large battle unit in the Roman army.

**massage** Rubbing muscles to help relax the body.

**mosaic** A picture made up of small pieces of coloured pottery, stone or glass.

**myth** An old story about gods, goddesses, heroes or monsters.

**offering** Something given to honour or please a god.

**slave** Someone who is not free, and is forced to work for no money.

**spirit** A magical being who brings good or bad luck.

**stola** A long pleated dress worn over a tunic.

**toga** A woollen robe worn by important men in Ancient Rome.

**trader** Someone who buys and sells goods to make money.

**tunic** A knee-length plain, sleeveless dress often worn by soldiers.

**villa** A large Roman house, usually in the countryside.

# INDEX